Contents

CW00411051

1

Preface

Many years ago, when I was a young Christian, I used to meet up with a Navigator friend, Bette. We chatted about all sorts of things, but we had little idea on what to do. Then in 1977 a couple visited the UK from Australia. Jack and May introduced us to a basic framework on how to grow in Jesus. This new discovery helped Bette and me in our times together. It also showed us how to help other Christians grow.

Over the years this framework has helped me when meeting up with others. It has also helped me to apply the biblical principle of 2 Timothy 2:2: "And the things you have heard me say in the presence of many witnesses entrust to reliable people who will also be qualified to teach others." Just as people taught us how to grow in Jesus, so we can teach others.

First Encounters is very much an 'essentials' booklet. So many other topics/issues could have been added. But, to start with, a new Christian needs the basics. I trust you find in this booklet what you are seeking, a guide to grow in authentic and vibrant faith.

Kathleen Blacklock

Introduction

Welcome to *First Encounters*! This is a study guide on how to grow as a young Christian. Please don't rush through it. If you feel challenged by a chapter, pause. Find additional material. Take as much time as you need.

This booklet can be used in groups, in pairs, or on your own. Here are a few guidelines...

A key to the symbols used in each chapter

A Bible fact ━━━━━━━━━━━━

A helpful pointer ━━━━━━━━━

A caution ━━━━━━━━━━━━

A choice ━━━━━━━━━━━━

Tips for working through this booklet with others

Meet regularly for an hour or so every week or fortnight. Arrange a specific time and date. Find a quiet place, a place where it is easy to talk and pray together.

Have materials handy – a cup of coffee or tea, a Bible, a notebook/journal and a pen.

A suggested schedule for your time together...

- (1 min) Pray to begin the session. Ask God's Holy Spirit to guide you.

- (10 - 15 min) Each share their concerns and joys since you last met. Pray for each other. Then practice your memory verses with each other.

- (40 min) Discuss the chapter, the issues arising, and how to apply it to your lives.

- (5 min) Pray for each other.

- (1 min) Put the next session in your diaries.

At the end of each chapter there is a Bible verse to memorise.

Practice these verses regularly. Here are a couple of suggestions how:

- Buy some index cards and write each verse on a card. Here is an example of how you could write it down (putting the reference at the beginning and the end will help you remember it):

  John 14:6 "Jesus answered, 'I am the way and the truth and the life. No one comes to the Father except through me.'" John 14:6

- Use a memory verse app: try The Bible Memory App, Verses – Bible Memory, or Bible Memory: Remember Me.

Encounter choice

The most important decision you can ever make is giving your life to God, believing that he is God and trusting in him. If you have done this, wow! Welcome to God's family! Welcome to the greatest adventure of your life!

Take some time to think about how you came to this decision. If you are meeting up with others, talk to them about what happened.

This chapter will help you unpack your life-altering decision. Read the Bible verses below and reflect on them. You will discover that turning to God means...

God exists.

The Bible says, "Without faith it is impossible to please God, because anyone who comes to him must believe that he exists and that he rewards those who earnestly seek him" (Hebrews 11:6). If you think about it, you can't come to God if you don't believe that he exists, and that he matters. By believing, you are saying, 'God is alive and well!'

What convinces you that God exists? What does this verse say about the God you now believe in? What does this say about you?

He loves you and wants a relationship with you.

The Bible also says, "See what great love the Father has lavished on us, that we should be called the children of God! And this is what we are!" (1 John 3:1). God loves you and invited you to be a part of his family. He wants to be your good and perfect Father. Other verses about God's love and being his child are 1 John 4:9 and John 1:12.

What does this verse say about you? What difference does it make to be a part of God's family? How do you think it will alter your life?

Before you believed, your relationship with God was messed up.

Our choices have consequences. The Bible reminds us, "But your iniquities have separated you from your God; your sins have hidden his face from you, so that he will not hear" (Isaiah 59:2). To explain, iniquities or sins are unfair or wrong behaviours, and these behaviours cut us off from God. So, even though God loves you, he also gave you the choice to say 'no' to him. You could choose to go your way or his. God offers his love and you decide.

How do you think God felt about you before you decided to follow him? Did you feel that God was hidden, that you were separated from him? What does it feel like now to be seen by God?

Saying 'yes' to Jesus means making Jesus the centre of your life.

The final step in becoming a part of God's family is so simple: "If you declare with your mouth, 'Jesus is Lord,' and believe in your heart that God raised him from the dead, you will be saved" (Romans 10:9). God sent his Son, Jesus, to remove the separation between you and God. He did it in the only way possible: he died for you, taking the punishment for your sins instead of you, so that God can offer you forgiveness and a new relationship with him. But that isn't all. Once you trust him, he becomes your Lord, your leader in life. He will guide and help you to become who you can be and to do what you can do.

What changed in your life when you realised what Jesus had done for you? What did you do as a result? How did you feel?

If on reading this you realise that you might not actually have said 'yes' to making Jesus the centre of your life, here is a prayer you might like to say:

'Dear God, thank you for loving me so much, even though I have lived life without you. Thank you for sending Jesus so he could remove the separation between me and you. I am sorry that I went my own way for so long. Please take me in as your child and help me to make Jesus the centre of my life. I want you to be my Father and to follow you for the rest of my life. Amen.'

Before you move on

Memorise Hebrews 11:6 and thank God for making you his child.

Hebrews 11:6 "Without faith it is impossible to please God, because anyone who comes to him must believe that he exists and that he rewards those who earnestly seek him." Hebrews 11:6

Encounter relationship

One good habit to start as a new Christian is to have a daily time of one-to-one with God. Many millions of Christians do it, taking time out to pray, read God's Word and listen to him. Being a part of God's family means learning to listen and relate to him.

It's possible to have a relationship with God.

God is approachable, and he wants to be approached. A poet in the Bible once prayed, "But as for me, it is good to be near God. I have made the Sovereign Lord my refuge; I will tell of all your deeds" (Psalm 73:28). You too can come near to God. You are precious to him and have the privilege of a relationship with him.

How do you feel about having a relationship with God? How did the poet feel about having a relationship with God? How does this poet's verse help you in your thinking?

It's a good idea.

Once you became a Christian, your new relationship with God began. And just like in any relationship, this new relationship takes time and energy to develop. King David in the Bible found time to be with God. He said, "In the morning, Lord, you hear my voice; in the morning I lay my requests before you and wait expectantly" (Psalm 5:3). King David's relationship with God was so important that, even in his busy life, he set aside time to meet with him.

Why do you think King David wanted to meet with God? What was involved in this relationship? Why was it so important? Would you be willing to spend time with God?

Don't put it off. Spend time with God regularly.

Sometimes it is easy to think that spending time with God is an option. But, just like in any relationship, you can't get close and understand a person if you don't spend time with them. Jesus took time out to spend time with God. The Bible says, "Very early in the morning, while it was still dark, Jesus got up, left the house and went off to a solitary place, where he prayed" (Mark 1:35). Just as with any special relationship, meeting with God will take effort.

As you consider Jesus's example, could you too set aside time to spend with God? Where could you find a quiet place, somewhere you wouldn't be disturbed and distracted?

Meet with God and find out his heart.

Just like when we chose to accept Jesus's invitation to be a child of God, we can also choose to let him influence the way we live. Jesus said this to some Christians in the Bible, "Here I am! I stand at the door and knock. If anyone hears my voice and opens the door, I will come in and eat with that person, and they with me" (Revelation 3:20). Jesus is calling us to have a relationship with him. Based on what he said to those Christians, here is a helpful way to start:

- **Go to the door:** Prepare your heart to spend time with Jesus. Ask his Holy Spirit to guide you as you meet with him. You could sing a song or read a psalm.

- **Open the door:** Open your heart by reading a short Bible passage, God's special letter to you. You could ask questions like 'What is God saying?', 'What does he mean?' A good place to start reading the Bible is Mark's Gospel.

- **Invite Jesus in:** Is there something you have read that speaks to your heart? Is there something in your life that God would like you to change, or do? Is there something he is showing you about himself? Record your thoughts in a notebook or journal.

- **Share a meal:** Spend time with these thoughts and ask God what you should do. Pray to him and ask for wisdom. Then, when you have time, follow through on your thoughts.

Remember, a relationship always takes time, but with persistence and the help of the Holy Spirit, your relationship with God will grow.

Before you move on

Memorise Revelation 3:20. Plan in some time to meet with God this week – try out different times to see what works best for you.

Revelation 3:20 "Here I am! I stand at the door and knock. If anyone hears my voice and opens the door, I will come in and eat with that person, and they with me." Revelation 3:20

Encounter
security

You are a brand-new child of God, but as the days go on, you might begin to wonder if you really are. You might feel wobbly in your heart. Maybe you think you didn't say the right words, or you're not worth it. Or you might have made some terrible mistakes and think that you're not good enough. Or maybe it is as simple as you can't pinpoint when you first started to believe. Look at the following verses; God has so much he wants to tell you.

God loved you even before you were thought of and born.

The Bible says, "For he [God] chose us in him before the creation of the world to be holy and blameless in his sight" (Ephesians 1:4). Even before you chose God, he chose you. He made the world and he made you. He even has a plan for your life! Another verse on God's everlasting love for you is Jeremiah 31:3.

How does it feel to know that God knew you and loved you even from before the world began? How does that change your view of God and yourself?

Nothing can separate you from God. Nothing!

The Bible is full of comforting verses and here is one of the most precious. It says, "For I am convinced that neither death nor life, neither angels nor demons, neither the present nor the future, nor any powers, neither height nor depth, nor anything else in all creation, will be able to separate us from the love of God that is in Christ Jesus our Lord" (Romans 8:38-39). It is a fact; God loves you. He wants you to know that Jesus is his gift to you. And when you accepted his sacrifice, he embraced you and won't let you go. You are safe!

What other things could you add to that list? Are there people or situations that could try to persuade you that this verse isn't true? How can you resist those lies and stand strong?

Doubt can stop you! The Holy Spirit moves in and reassures you.

Doubt is a feeling of uncertainty, but when it encounters reassuring facts, it will go away. The Bible is full of these reassuring facts. One is, "Because you are his sons [and daughters], God sent the Spirit of his Son into our hearts, the Spirit who calls out 'Abba, Father'" (Galatians 4:6). God's Holy Spirit, who comes to live in anyone who has become a Christian, convinces your heart and mind of the truth about God. He confirms in your heart that you are safe. Another reassuring verse is 1 John 5:11-12.

How can reading the Bible help settle your heart? How can the Holy Spirit help you to find peace and security? How can this change your attitude towards doubt?

you think this could settle your heart and help you feel secure in God? How can this certainty make a difference in your everyday life?

Before you move on

Memorise Ephesians 1:4. If you still have doubts about God's love for you, chat about this with a friend and pray together. Or thank God that nothing can snatch you out of his hands.

Ephesians 1:4 "For he chose us in him before the creation of the world to be holy and blameless in his sight." Ephesians 1:4

Believe it and receive it. You are God's child. You are safe.

Jesus said, "My sheep listen to my voice; I know them, and they follow me. I give them eternal life, and they shall never perish; no one will snatch them out of my hand" (John 10:27-28). God is with you, leading you. He is always speaking to you and protecting you. One way to help you remain strong in God is to keep spending time with him and following what he teaches you.

How can you make sure that you are spending time with God daily? How do

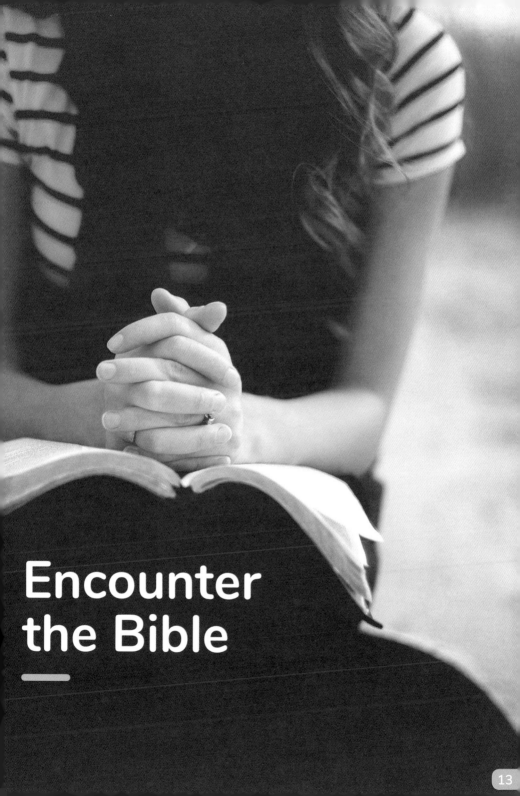

Encounter
the Bible

—

Did you know that the Bible has been translated into more than 680 different languages, and the New Testament has been translated into at least another 1530 languages? Why is this book so important?

God wants to communicate with you.

One great teacher, the Apostle Paul wrote, "All Scripture is God-breathed and is useful for teaching, rebuking, correcting and training in righteousness, so that the servant of God may be thoroughly equipped for every good work" (2 Timothy 3:16-17). Paul knew the importance of the Bible: it affected all areas of his life, and he wanted to share that fact with others.

From what the Apostle Paul says, why did he think the Bible was so important? How did he think it could affect lives? How does this change the way you think about the Bible?

It helps you understand how God wants you to live.

The Bible is also a personal book, with relevance for you and your life. "Whether you turn to the right or to the left, your ears will hear a voice behind you, saying, 'This is the way; walk in it'" (Isaiah 30:21). The Bible shapes your thinking and builds your confidence in God. And through the Holy Spirit, God highlights verses in the Bible that will help your decision-making, showing you the way to go and how to relate with others.

What questions do you have in your life right now? How do you think you can get to know the Bible so that you can be guided along your way?

It keeps you from going the wrong way.

The Bible is a guide in our everyday lives. It shows us what we need to do, or not to do, in order to live well. "How can a young person stay on the path of purity? By living according to your word" (Psalm 119:9). God cares about your wellbeing and had the Bible written to show you how to live. He gave the Holy Spirit to help you.

What are the challenges you face in life? Are there things that are dragging you down? How does this verse help you move forward? What choices can you make?

It is meant to be listened to and read.

Hear Matthew 7:24

Read Revelation 1:3

Study 2 Timothy 2:15

Memorise Deut. 5:1

Meditate Joshua 1:8

The Navigator **Bible Hand** is a helpful illustration of how to engage with the Bible, with each finger reminding you of a different aspect.

Hear

Jesus said, "Therefore everyone who hears these words of mine and puts them into practice is like a wise man who built his house on the rock" (Matthew 7:24). You can listen to the Bible when preachers preach it, or teachers teach it. You can also listen to the Bible online. Yet, within a day, most of us will forget what we hear. But hearing is a good start.

Study the Bible Hand diagram. Have you ever tried to balance a Bible using just your little finger? Try it. What else do you need to hold the Bible firmly in your hand, in your life?

Read

The Bible says, "Blessed is the one who reads aloud the words of this prophecy, and blessed are those who hear it and take to heart what is written in it, because the time is near" (Revelation 1:3). Reading the whole Bible, over time, is essential. Yet just hearing the Bible and reading it will only scratch the surface of God's deep wisdom.

Try balancing a Bible using just your two smallest fingers. It might be possible if you stand perfectly still. Now try to run. What does the verse in Revelation 1:3 say must be added to hearing and reading?

The other aspects of the Bible Hand will be covered in later sections. Some basic facts about the Bible can be found at the end of this booklet.

Before you move on

Memorise Matthew 7:24. If you haven't yet started reading through the Bible, find a Bible reading plan (see Practical Resources at the end of this booklet for ideas) and start today. And if you have started reading the Bible, take time to thank God for giving you his Word.

Matthew 7:24 "Therefore everyone who hears these words of mine and puts them into practice is like a wise man who built his house on the rock." Matthew 7:24

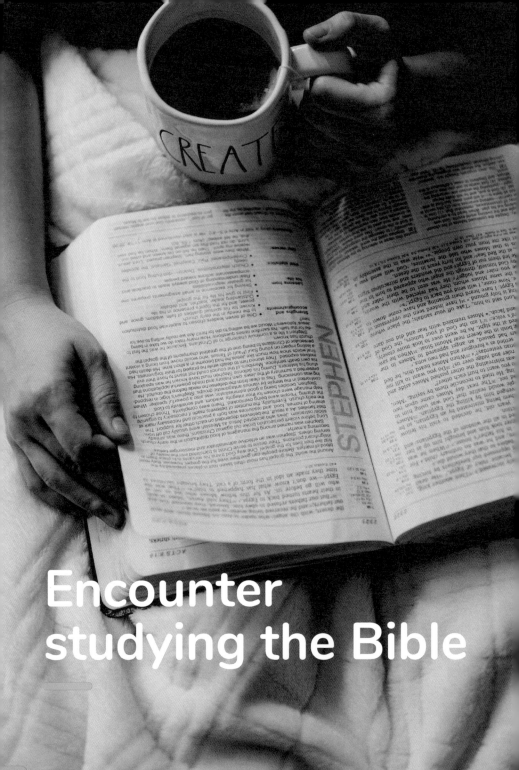

Encounter
studying the Bible

When you take time to dig deep and study the Bible, you will understand even more of what God wants you to know. And writing down these discoveries helps you remember them better. It is a fact that you take in more when you hear, read and study.

Hear Matthew 7:24

Read Revelation 1:3

Study 2 Timothy 2:15

Memorise Deut. 5:1

Meditate Joshua 1:8

God wants you to know for yourself what is true.

Some young Christians from Bible times dug deep into the Bible: "Now the Berean Jews were of more noble character than those in Thessalonica, for they received the message with great eagerness and examined the Scriptures every day to see if what Paul said was true" (Acts 17:11). These Bereans approached the Bible with a good attitude. They knew it was God's Word, so they could use it to figure out whether what people said was true.

Do you have questions that the Bible could help you answer? What did the Bereans do to help them know the truth? How can that apply to your life?

It enables you to be prepared and knowledgeable.

The Bible says, "Do your best to present yourself to God as one approved, a worker who does not need to be ashamed and who correctly handles the word of truth" (2 Timothy 2:15). It is an amazing thing: you can be your best and do your best when you know God's truth.

What does it mean to correctly handle truth? What would it look like if God's Word was mishandled? What do you think would be the consequences?

It stops you from misquoting the Bible or inadvertently changing it.

It is a scary thing to misquote the Bible. It is like putting words into God's mouth. Moses, a great leader once told God's people, "Do not add to what I command you and do not subtract from it, but keep the commands of the Lord your God that I give you" (Deuteronomy 4:2). Moses knew what it meant to want to change what God said, especially when God asked him to do something he didn't want to do. You can find this story in Exodus 3.

How can the warnings Moses gave be applied to your life? How can you ensure that you are understanding the Bible correctly? How can the Holy Spirit help you?

It will change your life.

A wise king once said, "My son, if you **accept** my words and store up my commands within you, turning your ear to wisdom and **apply**ing your heart to understanding – indeed, if you **call** out for insight and cry aloud for understanding, and if you look for it as for silver and **search** for it as for hidden treasure, then you will understand the fear of the Lord and find the knowledge of God" (Proverbs 2:1-5). Here is a simple guide on how to dig deep into any book of the Bible, based on these verses from Proverbs:

- **Call** out to God for him to give you insight and understanding through his Holy Spirit.

- **Search** for the treasure – ask questions like Who? Why? What? Where? When?

- **Accept** with an open heart what is written in the passage.

- **Apply** it – how can this passage change my life? My attitudes? My values? My relationships? My heart for God? My goals?

There may be topics or life issues you would like to explore. You may be wondering what the Bible has to say about them. You may find it helpful to search for the topic at www.biblegateway.com or www.biblehub.com. Or chat with a friend or those you are working through this booklet with.

Before you move on

Memorise 2 Timothy 2:15. Choose a chapter in the Bible, maybe John chapter 9. Print it out, using one of the websites above. Go through the steps mentioned above and write, highlight or underline as you go.

2 Timothy 2:15 "Do your best to present yourself to God as one approved, a worker who does not need to be ashamed and who correctly handles the word of truth." 2 Timothy 2:15

Encounter memorising and meditating

Using the picture of the Bible Hand, it is still difficult to hold a Bible with only three fingers. Adding the other two fingers will give us a much better grip. When you look at Jesus's life, you can see how essential it is to memorise and meditate (think deeply about rather than emptying your mind) on verses from the Bible. When Jesus was alone in the desert and was tempted, he didn't have a Bible with him. Yet, he could stand strong. "It is written..." he kept saying (Matthew 4:4-10). Jesus knew his Bible by heart and it protected him.

Hear Matthew 7:24

Read Revelation 1:3

Study 2 Timothy 2:15

Memorise Deut. 5:1

Meditate Joshua 1:8

Memorising verses by heart gives immediate access to the Bible.

The Bible encourages us to know God's Word. One day "Moses summoned all Israel and said: 'Hear, Israel, the decrees and the laws I declare in your hearing today. Learn them and be sure to follow them" (Deuteronomy 5:1). Memorising the Bible gives you a secure foundation in life. It enables you to recall God's Word accurately in every situation.

Are there creative ways you can memorise God's Word? How can you enable it to not only sit in your mind, but change your heart?

Memorising enables you to meditate on the Bible anywhere.

The Apostle Paul wrote, "Let the message of Christ dwell among you richly as you teach and admonish one another with all wisdom through psalms, hymns, and songs from the Spirit, singing to God with gratitude in your hearts" (Colossians 3:16). When we memorise the Bible, we can know how to live. And if we go from memorising to meditating, it can totally change our lives.

What are the results when we memorise God's Word? What is the attitude we should have to the Word of God?

Meditating on the Bible will help you fight temptation.

There is nothing good about temptation. A poet in the Bible prayed, "I have hidden your word in my heart that I might not sin against you" (Psalm 119:11). Temptations will hit you at the most unexpected times. God's Word really is the antidote, and as you follow God, he will give you the strength to stand strong.

What other ways do you think knowing the Bible can help you in life? How can it give you strength to do what is right?

Meditating on the Bible will help you live as God wants.

God told one young leader, "Keep this Book of the Law always on your lips; meditate on it day and night, so that you may be careful to do everything written in it. Then you will be prosperous and successful" (Joshua 1:8). Meditation is essential in learning to live out a vibrant faith. Here are some suggestions on how to memorise and meditate:

- **Write out a verse and read it slowly.** Emphasise different words or phrases, asking the Holy Spirit to lead you.

- **Ask questions** about the verse. What does this mean to me? What is God saying?

- **Read the verses that come before and after the verse you have chosen.** What is the context? What is the message you are hearing? Can you find any other verses that are similar?

- **Above all, ask God how you can APPLY the verse to your life.**

Using the picture of the Bible Hand, you will notice that you can hold the Bible using just your thumb and forefinger. If life is busy, these two aspects of the Bible Hand – memorising and meditating – are the ones that will impact you the most. Yet the fullest way to understand is to **Hear**, **Read**, **Study**, **Memorise** and **Meditate**.

As you continue to memorise new Bible verses, don't forget to practise the verses you have already learnt.

Before you move on

Memorise Joshua 1:8. Thank God for his Holy Spirit, who helps you change. Set some time aside to meditate on this verse.

Joshua 1:8 "Keep this Book of the Law always on your lips; meditate on it day and night, so that you may be careful to do everything written in it. Then you will be prosperous and successful." Joshua 1:8

Encounter
prayer

Prayer is communicating with God as part of your relationship with him. You can talk to him as your caring Father and you can tell him your needs, joys and concerns. You can do it anyway you like: quietly in your heart, or out loud, or even by writing it down in a notebook or journal.

God wants to hear from you.

God really wants to hear from you. In the Bible he tells you, "Call to me and I will answer you and tell you great and unsearchable things you do not know" (Jeremiah 33:3). God loves you and he is patient. He waits for you to speak. Other verses on God wanting to hear from us are Psalm 91:15 and Ephesians 3:20.

How do you feel when you think of God wanting to hear from you? How does this affect your relationship with him? What could you tell him?

He wants you to communicate with him throughout the day.

The Apostle Paul indicated God's desire when he wrote to some believers to urge them to "pray continually" (1 Thessalonians 5:17). Praying to God isn't a something that you do a couple of times a year; it is part of a believer's daily lifestyle.

What does this verse mean to you? How do you think you could remember to pray to God throughout the day? What concerns would you bring to him?

Prayer is a place of humility before God.

Jesus knew that praying can be misused. In his day, some people used it as a power play to show others how spiritual they were. The same can be true today, so Jesus gives some important advice: "But when you pray, go into your room, close the door and pray to your Father, who is unseen. Then your Father, who sees what is done in secret, will reward you" (Matthew 6:6). Whether you are praying on your own or with others, you are invited to come to God with deep respect and humility.

How can you show this humility before God? How can you maintain it while praying with others in a group or in pairs?

Prayer is working with God for his will to happen in your life.

Jesus gave his followers an example of how to pray, which has become known as the Lord's Prayer. This is recorded in Matthew 6:9-13. It is only fifty-three words long, yet it is so profound. Let's take a deeper look.

The Navigator **Prayer Hand** will help you here. Prayer is much more than making personal requests. It is about relating fully with God.

Praise Psalm 105:1

Thanks 1 Thes. 5:18

Others 1 Samuel 12:23

Self John 16:24

Sorry 1 John 1:9

Praise

In the Lord's Prayer Jesus showed what it means to praise God. He prayed, "Our Father in heaven, hallowed be your name" (Matthew 6:9). Jesus wants us to remember how wonderful God is and for us to tell him. Psalm 105:1 says, "Give praise to the Lord, proclaim his name; make known among the nations what he has done." Another helpful verse about praise is Psalm 113:3.

Think of the ways in which you have experienced how wonderful God is. In Psalm 31:21-22, King David was able to praise God even in challenging times. Why do you think it is so important to tell God how much we appreciate him? What does it do for our own hearts?

Thanks

In the Lord's Prayer Jesus prayed, "Your kingdom come, your will be done, on earth as it is in heaven" (Matthew 6:10). As the Apostle Paul reminds us in 1 Thessalonians 5:18, God's will for us involves being

thankful: "Give thanks in all circumstances; for this is God's will for you in Christ Jesus." God is in control of everything. He will always be, and no one can intimidate him or stop him. We can thank him for who he is and what he does. Another helpful verse is Ephesians 5:20.

Have you experienced something good in your life? Or in the lives of others? Take time to thank God. Also, thank him for who you are – he made you without any mistakes. Why do you think God wants thankfulness to be a part of our lives?

Before you move on

Memorise the Lord's prayer in Matthew 6:9-13. Spend some time this week thanking and praising him.

Matthew 6:9-13 "This, then, is how you should pray: 'Our Father in heaven, hallowed be your name, your kingdom come, your will be done, on earth as it is in heaven. Give us today our daily bread. And forgive us our debts, as we also have forgiven our debtors. And lead us not into temptation but deliver us from the evil one.'" Matthew 6:9-13

Encounter
praying for
others and yourself

The wonder of prayer is that you can pray about anything, and that includes yourself and others. It isn't selfish to go to God with your needs or the needs of those you care about. He wants to hear from you and he wants to answer. In the Lord's Prayer, Jesus prayed, "Give us today our daily bread" (Matthew 6:11). The word 'us' includes everyone, even you.

Praise Psalm 105:1

Thanks 1 Thes. 5:18

Others 1 Samuel 12:23

Self John 16:24

Sorry 1 John 1:9

Praying for change is possible because God can do anything.

Jesus gives us the courage to pray. He says, "I will do whatever you ask in my name, so that the Father may be glorified in the Son. You may ask me for anything in my name, and I will do it" (John 14:13-14). He also said, "You did not choose me, but I chose you and appointed you so that you might go and bear fruit – fruit that will last – and so that whatever you ask in my name the Father will give you" (John 15:16). When we pray, anything is possible because God is all powerful!

What is on your heart? What needs do you have? What are the needs of those you care about? Or even your enemies? You can pray for them too!

Praying with the Holy Spirit is essential so that you can pray what is good.

The Apostle Paul made an important point about prayer: "Pray in the Spirit on all occasions with all kinds of prayers and requests. With this in mind, be alert and always keep on praying for all the Lord's people" (Ephesians 6:18). It could be easy to ask for things that might not be for the best without realising it. For this reason it is important to ask God to guide you through his Holy Spirit. If you feel uneasy about something you want to pray, then stop. Another helpful verse is Romans 8:26.

How can the Bible help you know what are good prayers? How can the Lord's Prayer help you? How can the Holy Spirit be involved in these decisions?

You don't have to feel unsure about praying for others.

Samuel, a prophet and teacher in the Bible, told a crowd of people, "As for me, far be it from me that I should sin against the Lord by failing to pray for you" (1 Samuel 12:23). Samuel knew the importance of praying for others. Other helpful verses are Colossians 1:9 and Ephesians 1:17.

Do you need wisdom in how to pray for others? What are their needs, desires and struggles? Look at the extra verses above; how can the Holy Spirit help you in your prayers for other people?

God wants you to be bold in your prayers.

Jesus said something amazing about prayer: "Until now you have not asked for anything in my name. Ask and you will receive, and your joy will be complete" (John 16:24). Another helpful verse is 1 John 5:14-15. This applies not only when we pray for others; God also wants us to pray for ourselves. A relationship involves asking and receiving.

There will be some prayers that we see God act on immediately, whereas for some prayers it may might take a while before we see the answer. There are some prayers that God won't act on, but even that is an answer. He loves you and knows what is best for you. Think of your needs, desires and struggles, and be bold as you pray for yourself.

Before you move on

Memorise John 16:24. You might also like to keep a notebook or journal of your prayers, then when God answers them you can record the answers too. It will really encourage you.

John 16:24 "Until now you have not asked for anything in my name. Ask and you will receive, and your joy will be complete." John 16:24

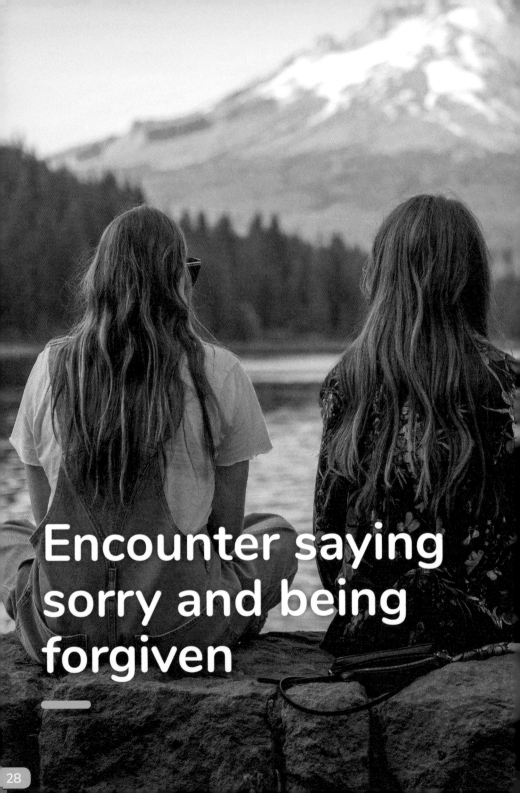

Encounter saying sorry and being forgiven

The last aspect of the Prayer Hand is maybe the hardest, but God doesn't want us to avoid it.

Praise Psalm 105:1

Thanks 1 Thes. 5:18

Others 1 Samuel 12:23

Self John 16:24

Sorry 1 John 1:9

In the Lord's Prayer, Jesus added this statement: "Forgive us our debts, as we also have forgiven our debtors" (Matthew 6:12). Debts refers to sins, and debtors are those who hurt us. Everyone has messed up somewhere, and needs to be forgiven. And everyone has been hurt and needs the grace and courage to forgive.

God sent Jesus to make it possible for your sins to be forgiven.

No one can even come close to making amends to God for the wrong things they have done. But Jesus, who did not sin, offers to take the punishment we deserve so we can be forgiven. God loves you so much that he willingly gave Jesus his Son to rescue us: "For God so loved the world that he gave his one and only Son, that whoever believes in him shall not perish but have eternal life" (John 3:16).

What does God's forgiveness of you depend on? What are the implications of this? What does this mean for you when you mess up?

God wants you to be honest.

Sometimes your sins might be embarrassing, and you might want to hide them from God, from others, and even from yourself. The Bible says this isn't a wise thing to do: "If we claim to be without sin, we deceive ourselves and the truth is not in us" (1 John 1:8). In the end, you are only fooling yourself.

Why is it important to be honest about who you are inside? How could pretending to be perfect affect the way we receive forgiveness from God? What would help you be honest before God?

When you hide your sins, you hurt yourself.

Often people think that God will never see what they do, and if they hide it well enough they will get away with it. But everything we do always has a consequence. The Bible says, "Whoever conceals their sins does not prosper, but the one who confesses and renounces them finds mercy" (Proverbs 28:13). God's solution is so simple – we need to acknowledge that we sin and say sorry to God, and he can then help us live differently. Another helpful verse is Romans 3:23.

What could be some consequences of trying to hide your sins from God? What would that do to your heart?

It is good to acknowledge your sins and say sorry.

When you put your trust in what Jesus has done for you on the cross you are forgiven and welcomed into God's family. But this doesn't mean you won't sin again. Inevitably you will, but this doesn't change God's love for you or mean that you are no longer a Christian. Saying sorry for your sins helps you to acknowledge your need for Jesus and will help you change how you behave. And God has given us a wonderful promise: "If we confess our sins, he is faithful and just and will forgive us our sins and purify us from all unrighteousness" (1 John 1:9). Saying sorry can be summarised in five steps:

- **Recognise** what has been done wrong. Ask the Holy Spirit to open your heart.

- **Confess** it to God and, if appropriate, to the person who has been hurt.

- **Ask** for forgiveness from God and, if appropriate, from the one who was hurt.

- **Turn away** from doing wrong, and if possible, make amends.

- **Accept** that you are forgiven. You can move on.

Take some time to consider your life. Is there something you need to say sorry to God for? Have you hurt someone, even if you didn't mean to? Apologise to God and, if appropriate, to the person you hurt. Remember, the Prayer Hand is essential if you want to grow in God.

In the Lord's Prayer, Jesus linked asking for forgiveness with forgiving others. It may be that someone has hurt or wronged you or someone you love. How can knowing that you are forgiven by God help you to forgive other people?

Before you move on

Memorise 1 John 1:9. Set some time aside to ask God to show you where you need to say sorry to him or to forgive someone. Thank God for his incredible gift of forgiveness.

1 John 1:9 "If we confess our sins, he is faithful and just and will forgive us our sins and purify us from all unrighteousness." 1 John 1:9

Encounter God's help in temptation

Difficulties will come, sometimes through things outside of your control and sometimes as a result of the choices you make. These challenges can produce temptations, but God can help.

So, what is temptation? The dictionary definition is 'the desire to do something, especially something unwise or wrong'. It is the urge to reject God's way and go your own way, the attitude of doing your own thing and ignoring what God wants. And, sadly, anyone can feel tempted.

God protects us even when temptation comes.

The Apostle Paul said, "No temptation has overtaken you except what is common to mankind. And God is faithful; he will not let you be tempted beyond what you can bear. But when you are tempted, he will also provide a way out so that you can endure it" (1 Corinthians 10:13). Everyone experiences times when they desperately want to do the wrong thing and there is a struggle inside them over it.

How does it help you to know that everyone faces similar problems? What kind of help does God provide for you to enable you to withstand temptation?

You can fight temptation God's way.

In the Lord's Prayer, Jesus shows us that we should talk to God about temptation. In his prayer, Jesus said, "And lead us not into temptation, but deliver us from the evil one" (Matthew 6:13). When we communicate with God about temptation, whatever the difficulties we are facing, he can help us and give us the strength to overcome it.

How does prayer enable you to resist the urge to do something wrong? How does the Bible help you stay strong? How can you rely on the Holy Spirit to help?

Everyone has weaknesses, but it is easy to pretend to be strong.

In fighting temptation, it is good to study your life. The Bible says, "Each person is tempted when they are dragged away by their own evil desire and enticed" (James 1:14). It is important to know what areas of life you find difficult. Once you know that, you will be able to find constructive ways to avoid temptation. You may find the story of Joseph in Genesis 39:1-12 helpful.

What areas of life do you find challenging? How can you recognise temptation?

You can resist temptation by being vigilant and praying.

Just before Jesus died, his helpers were with him, but they kept falling asleep. Jesus told them how to fight temptation: "Watch and pray so that you will not fall into temptation. The spirit is willing, but the flesh is weak" (Matthew 26:41). Temptation is part of life, but with God there is a secure way through.

Here are some practical steps to overcome temptation:

- If you see temptation coming, if possible, **get away**. Find ways to avoid it.

- Keep **memorising** and **meditating** on Bible verses. They will give you strength and courage.

- **Pray** for protection.

- Get **support** from a friend to help you stay strong.

What are some ways you can avoid temptation? How can knowing Bible verses by heart help you in fighting temptation? Why is prayer so important in resisting temptation?

Before you move on

Memorise 1 Corinthians 10:13. Thank God for always being with you and helping you resist temptation. And if you don't have a friend who can help you stay strong, pray and see if there is someone you could ask. You might be able to help them in return.

1 Corinthians 10:13 "No temptation has overtaken you except what is common to mankind. And God is faithful; he will not let you be tempted beyond what you can bear. But when you are tempted, he will also provide a way out so that you can endure it." 1 Corinthians 10:13

Encounter sharing your God-story

One of the most amazing stories you have is how you became a Christian. God doesn't want you to keep it hidden — he wants you to share it with others. As you tell them what happened to you, it just might spark their interest in God as well.

God wants you to share your story.

Jesus helped a man who was having a tough time. Afterwards, when this man wanted to follow him, Jesus said, "Go home to your own people and tell them how much the Lord has done for you, and how he has had mercy on you'" (Mark 5:19). This man took a brave step. He went back to his home, where everyone knew him. His story changed many lives.

Who are the people in your life that you could tell your story to? What are the things God has done for you? How has he shown you mercy?

Your story is unique to you.

God will help you tailor your story, so that bridges can be built between those listening and God. The Apostle Paul understood this challenge. He said, "Pray also for me, that whenever I speak, words may be given me so that I will fearlessly make known the mystery of the gospel" (Ephesians 6:19). Even though Paul was a

brave person, he knew that he needed help from God when he spoke.

What is your story? What is the message you would like to share? Who can you ask to help you with suggestions and in prayer?

Don't be afraid to share your God-story.

Jesus knew it would be a challenge to share about our faith and it is so easy to hide our story and not tell anyone. To encourage us, he said, "Neither do people light a lamp and put it under a bowl. Instead they put it on its stand, and it gives light to everyone in the house. In the same way, let your light shine before others, that they may see your good deeds and glorify your Father in heaven" (Matthew 5:15-16).

Why is it so important to tell others your story? In what ways can you take your story out of hiding and let it shine to others?

You can learn how to do it from the best.

Take a few minutes to read the Apostle Paul's story of how he became a Christian in Acts 22:2-21. Here are some ideas from Paul's story:

- What were you like before you became a Christian? Give examples.

Or if you can't remember when you became a Christian, how were you aware of him in your life?

- What was it that drew you to Jesus? Be specific. What happened at the point when you agreed in your heart that you wanted to follow Jesus for the rest of your life? Or was there a decision you had to make - maybe choosing between God and what you wanted?

- What is life like now?

Here are some more ideas for when you share your story:

- Keep it short – 3 to 5 minutes is fine.

- Keep it real and centred on God, not just about yourself.

- Keep it focused – sometimes just a part of your story is enough.

- Keep listening to God – every person we meet will have different needs.

Remember, just as we are God's precious children, so is everyone else in the world. They just don't know it. After you have shared your story, some might reject it but others might show an interest. Don't stop there. Continue to talk with them about faith and what it means to be a believer in Jesus. You may feel God prompting you to ask them if they would like to give their life to Jesus. If they would, be ready with a prayer to share with them.

And, if they do pray for Jesus to come into their lives, maybe you could read *First Encounters* with them and help them grow as a new Christian!

Before you move on

Memorise Mark 5:19. Write out your story and pray for opportunities to share it with others.

Mark 5:19 "Jesus did not let him, but said, 'Go home to your own people and tell them how much the Lord has done for you, and how he has had mercy on you.'" Mark 5:19

Encounter being a disciple of Jesus

In his parting words to his followers, Jesus said, "Go and make disciples" (Matthew 28:19). So, what is a disciple? It comes from a Greek word *mathetes*, which means an apprentice, pupil or learner. Jesus wanted those he apprenticed to grow in God and follow him. He also wanted them to teach others what they had learned.

God is honoured when you grow.

Jesus had his sights set on what was important. He said to his followers, "This is to my Father's glory, that you bear much fruit, showing yourselves to be my disciples" (John 15:8). And Jesus didn't expect his disciples to just know how to grow – he taught them over three amazing years. Then they could show others how to do it.

What do you think Jesus meant by bearing fruit? Read Galatians 5:22-23. How does bearing fruit show that you are growing as a disciple?

Jesus invites you to rearrange your life for him.

Following Jesus is not to be taken lightly. Just as he gave everything to make you a part of God's family, he would like the same commitment from you. He said, "Whoever wants to be my disciple must deny themselves and take up their cross and follow me" (Matthew 16:24). Another helpful verse is Luke 14:33.

What things might be holding you back from following Jesus? What fears? What people? How can you entrust these things to God?

Growing in Jesus doesn't happen in a vacuum.

Growing in Jesus isn't easy on your own. You will need others to encourage you as you grow in faith. In Acts 14:21-22 it says, "They returned... strengthening the disciples and encouraging them to remain true to the faith." Believers need each other to remain strong, and you will find that encouragement goes a long way to help you grow.

How can you find people who will encourage you in your faith? How can you encourage others to remain strong in God?

Jesus said that doing his will is essential to being his follower.

Jesus said, "If you hold to my teaching, you are really my disciples" (John 8:31). Another helpful verse is John 13:35. Growing in Jesus happens when you know what Jesus says. The best way to do this is by studying the Bible, God's Word. The best place to do it is with others. And God's Holy Spirit will help you (John 14:26). And the things you learn you can then you can pass on (Matthew 28:20).

How could meeting up in pairs or groups help you to grow in Jesus? You could find a group to join or start your own! How can the Holy Spirit help you in your growth?

Before you finish this booklet

Memorise John 8:31. Thank God that he wants you to grow in following him. Thank him for the people in your life who can help you grow and change.

John 8:31 "To the Jews who believed him, Jesus said, 'If you hold to my teaching, you are really my disciples.'"
John 8:31

Basic facts about the Bible

The Bible...

- is divided into two parts:

  - the Old Testament starts at the creation of the world and ends with the Jewish people waiting for the promised Messiah.

  - the New Testament starts with the birth of Jesus and ends with a description of the future return of Jesus to earth.

- contains 66 different books, 39 in the Old Testament and 27 in the New Testament.

- was written by many authors and over about 1600 years.

- was originally written in three languages: Hebrew, Aramaic and Greek.

- was first translated into English by John Wycliffe in 1382.

- can be summed up in 15 words: God loves us and wants a relationship. The only way is through Jesus, his Son.

Practical resources

Other Navigator books

Time Out with God by Brian Blacklock – a booklet on how to have one-to-one time with God.
The Art of Leading a Small Group by Tom Ringrose – a booklet on how to lead a Bible study group.
Godfulness by Derek Leaf – a booklet on how to meditate on the Bible.
Bible Reading Plan by Derek Leaf – a plan to help you read the whole Bible over 1, 2 or 3 years.
Bridge to Life – a short leaflet on how to become a Christian.
Living the Conversation by Holly Price - a booklet on how to share your faith with others.

Order online at navigators.co.uk/online-shop

Websites with discipleship resources

www.navigators.co.uk/resources
www.beingrecreated.org

Websites to help in studying the Bible and finding Bible verses

www.biblehub.com
www.biblegateway.com

An app to help you pray

PrayerMate

Apps to help in memorising Bible verses

The Bible Memory App
Verses – Bible Memory
Bible Memory: Remember Me

About the authors

Kathleen Blacklock and her husband Brian have helped many people find God and grow in him. For 30 years they worked with the Navigators UK, leading student ministries in the UK and Canada. They have also served on many leadership teams. Kath and Brian currently live in the UK and have three grown sons.

Eva Leaf coordinates the Navigators UK publications team and writes for children and adults. She and her husband Derek are also on the Navigators UK leadership team.